Dedication :

To all my Rice relatives, my mother Anita Rice, and my grandparents Holland and Ruth England Rice. A special thanks to my Aunt Mickey and Linda for sharing all their wonderful stories.

Forward

Discovering our own family history is so important for so many reasons. It gives us a sense of where we came from and who we are. We are the pieces of all who came before us.

Our ancestors lived remarkable lives and were brave enough to leave their homelands in foreign countries and come to America to start over. They settled this country, raised families, went through wars, disease and constant change. They were remarkable people in a new land called America and paved the way for many of the things we hold dear – constitutional rights, freedom of religion and speech, education, morals, values, attitudes and belief systems. We inherited all of these from our various ancestors.

We are also a true mix of many different races, cultures and religions. Our ancestors did come from foreign countries all over the world and some were already here as Native American Indians. Once they got to America they married people from different backgrounds, races and cultures. America is truly a "melting pot".

Please note I do not claim complete accuracy of the information in this book. There are many discrepancies throughout the historical records, census records, etc. This is correct to the best of my knowledge.

Other names in this book: England, Perkins, Smith, Harwell, Bingham, Joette, Bullock, Relms, Hewes, Hussey, Trant, Whyte, Wall.

The RICE Name

Rice was originally Ryss and of Welsh origin. There are two origins for the Rice name. One is native Gaelic derivation meaning "a branch". In another translation is means "fiery warrior". The other origin is from the southern province of Munster of Welsh origin from "ap Rhys" literally "the son of Rhys". The "ap" denoted nobility or distinction. In the 14th century Rice families were in Limerick and Kerry. They were mayors, sheriffs and gentry in Dingle. They were involved with the Jacobite cause and during the 17th century many Rice's lost their lands as a result of the Cromwellian forfeitures.

The Rice History

The Rice's were amongst the first of the Anglo-Norman and Welsh settlers who came over to Ireland with Robert Fitz-Stephen in 1169. The name which is undoubtedly one of Welsh origin, is traceable in Ireland almost from the earliest period of existing records, but more especially in Kerry.

The first settlers of the family in Ireland were most probably relatives of descendants of Griffith Ap Rhys, of Newton, one of the ancient Princes of South Wales. In 1501-1502 the Prince of Wales and his bride Princess Catherine went to Ludlow Castle, they were greeted by Welsh Lords headed by Sir Rhys ap Thomas (King Henry's "father Rhys") he gave Catherine his son, Griffith Ap Rhys, to be gentleman usher and Welsh Interpreter and as his Mother was Mary daughter of Thomas Howard Earl Duke of Norfolk, the Rices may perhaps claim descent from the Royal House of Plantagenet.

They soon relinquished, it seems, the old Welsh patronymic "Ap" and adopted the Anglo-Norman "Fitz" instead. The majority of Fitz-Stephen's followers were nearly all his own countrymen, and of course, it was only natural that they would sooner follow the customs and habits of their comrades in arms than those of he natives of their adopted country. After a time, then the name Fitz-Rhyz" came to be written "Fitz Rice". However they retained it for a much longer time than the old Welsh "Ap" for we find that three of the Dingle Rices, bearing the Christian name FitzDominick" appeared as claimants for land after the Restoration.

The surname Rice is purely Welsh, the original form having been either Rhys or Ap Rhys (i.e. Rice of "son of" Rice). And we also find in old documents and records the same name under different forms, such as Rhys, Reisch, Reis, etc.

The Rice's have a direct line to William the Conqueror (1028). Other

Some interesting Rice family history comes out in Dingle, Ireland during the French Revolution. James Louis Rice was a friend with Emperor James II of Austria. He was the son of Black Tom Rice and they were wine traders. They lived in the "Rice House". James Louis was educated in Belgium and joined the Austrian army. The Emperor Joseph II of Austria was the brother of Marie Antoinette, the queen of France. She was being held prisoner in the Temple in Paris with her husband and children. The French Revolution was in full swing. Thomas Rice and the Emperor devised a plan to rescue Marie from the Temple and hide her out in Dingle Ireland until the war had passed. The story says they went to get her and she refused to go. She did not want to leave her husband, the King and leave her children behind. So she stayed and accepted her fate of death. As history tells us, she was beheaded.

The Rice Family

There are three Rice lines in America. One is the Deacon Edmund Rice family from Massachusetts, the second line is the County Bucks of Ireland and the third is the Rice's of Virginia and North Carolina. My line is the Rice's of Virginia, Caswell Co, NC and then on to West Tennessee.

This book contains the Rice Family History from Edward Rice (1495) in Dingle Ireland to first immigrant Thomas Rice, born in England in 1650 to the current Rice families in West Tennessee in 1997. This is eighteen generations of Riches. The Rice families were in Virginia, then NC and split off into Tennessee, Kentucky and Texas. My direct Rice relatives lived in Savannah, TN and Sardis and Memphis TN. Also included are some of the Rices from Virginia, North Carolina, South Carolina and Texas.

Famous Rice's include South Carolina preacher Rev. Amaziah Rice. Rev David Rice of Kentucky is known as the Father of Presbyterianism and the Apostle of Kentucky. John Rice and his brothers were well known Indian traders in the Nashville area. Also related are the famous playwright Tennessee Williams.

My Rice Line

My ancestor, Thomas Rice came from England to America in 1680. Over the next three hundred years they were landowners, farmers, businessmen. They moved from Virginia to NC and then split up into branches that settled all over the country. The Rice families went to South Carolina (around Anderson), Texas, Kentucky, Illinois and my line eventually came to West Tennessee. Many Rice men fought in various wars and some died. Most of the Rice women lived to be old and productive.

While doing my research on the Rice line I stumbled across the South Carolina line of Rice's while I was living in Greenville, SC. An hour away was the town where they lived for many generations, Belton, SC and the old Rice cemetery. There on a lonely hilltop was a small family cemetery with the graves of my great, great, great grandparents and relatives. The cemetery was isolated and far into the countryside and by sheer coincidence I found it one day.

The Rice Family Cemetery in Belton, SC

MY DIRECT ANCESTRAL GENEOLOGY

GENERATION 18:
Edward Rice and Ann Wall
1495-1523 Dingle Ireland

GENERATION 17:
Robert Rice and Julianna Whyte
1518-1569   Dingle, Ireland

GENERATION 16:
Stephen Rice and Helen Trant
1540-1623 Dingle, Ireland / Helen 1542-1565

GENERATION 15:
Dominick Rice and Alice Hussey
1564-   Dingle, Ireland

GENERATION 14:
Richard Rice and Ann Cooper
1588-1657 Dingle Ireland

GENERATION 13:
Sir Stephen Rice and Abigail
1637-1715 Ireland

GENERATION 12:
Thomas Rice and Any Marcy Hewes
1650-1711 Shirementon Bristol, England to Virginia USA

GENERATION 11:
William Rice and Elizabeth Relms
1686-1733   Virginia to Hanover County, NC

GENERATION 10:
    Benejah Rice and Mary
    1710-1746 Beufort, NC

GENERATION 9:
    Hezekiah Rice and Mary Bullock
    1739-1796 Albermarle Co, VA to Caswell Co, NC

GENERATION 8:
    Jeptha Rice and Nancy Joette
    1758-1820 Albermarle Co, VA to Sumner Co, TN

GENERATION 7:
    William Rice and Nancy Bingham
    1803-1859 Caswell County, NC to TN

GENERATION 6:
    Joseph Rice and Martha Jane Harwell
    1837-1867 Hardin County, TN (Savannah and Sardis)

GENERATION 5:
    William Henry Rice and Elizabeth Smith
    1862-1924 Henderson County, TN – Sardis
    1862-1925

GENERATION 4:
    Charles Walter Rice and Zona Perkins
    1886-1973 Sardis, TN

GENERATION 3:
    Oral Holland Rice and Ruth England Rice
    1911-1993 Sardis, TN to Humboldt, TN

GENERATION 2:
Margaret Anita Rice Fletcher
1936-   Savannah, TN to Asheville, NC

GENERATION 1: Katherine Fletcher (the author of this book)

THE LIVES OF MY RICE ANCESTORS

GENERATION ONE:

The author of this book, Katherine Fletcher

GENERATION TWO:

Margaret Anita Rice married Hayes Fentress Fletcher
Their Children:
- John Marc Fletcher
- Suzanne Ruth Fletcher
- Katherine Grace Fletcher
- Grant Wesley Fletcher

My story starts with my mother, Margaret Anita Rice Fletcher.   Here is her biography in her own words:

Margaret Anita Rice was born on December 3, 1936, to Margaret Ruth England Rice and Oral Holland Rice, in Sardis, Tennessee. Anita was later joined by two sisters, Linda Jane and Mickey Dianne. She and Linda were both delivered by Ruth's Uncle Gib, a country doctor who made his rounds by wagon. Moving to Memphis as a child was an adventure, safely cocooned within the close and loving family circle. Good schools and a supportive church, with all their activities, filled her life, along with piano lessons and listening to radio dramas.

Leaving Memphis to attend Lambuth College in Jackson, TN, proved to be a path that influenced the rest of her life. For there, in Lambuth's bookstore, she met her future husband, Hayes Fletcher. Their four children were born during his years in the ministry, 15 busy and fulfilling years. Leaving the Chicago area for the New York area was at first sad, but quickly becoming exciting as new possibilities unfolded. Included among them was the opportunity to attend the NY School of Interior Design.

After five years, they moved the family back South, after having lived away for 20 years. Anita began a retail career with Kirkland's, Inc. that lasted for 20 years, and stimulated growth from wearing many "hats" on the job. In retirement, Anita and Hayes moved to Asheville, NC, to enjoy the mountains and the rich crafts heritage of the area. Weaving and dabbling in all things fiber-related, plus making new friends, plus celebrating 53+ years of marriage, makes her a happy camper.

Ancestors of Oral Holland Rice

Parents | Grandparents | Great-Grandparents

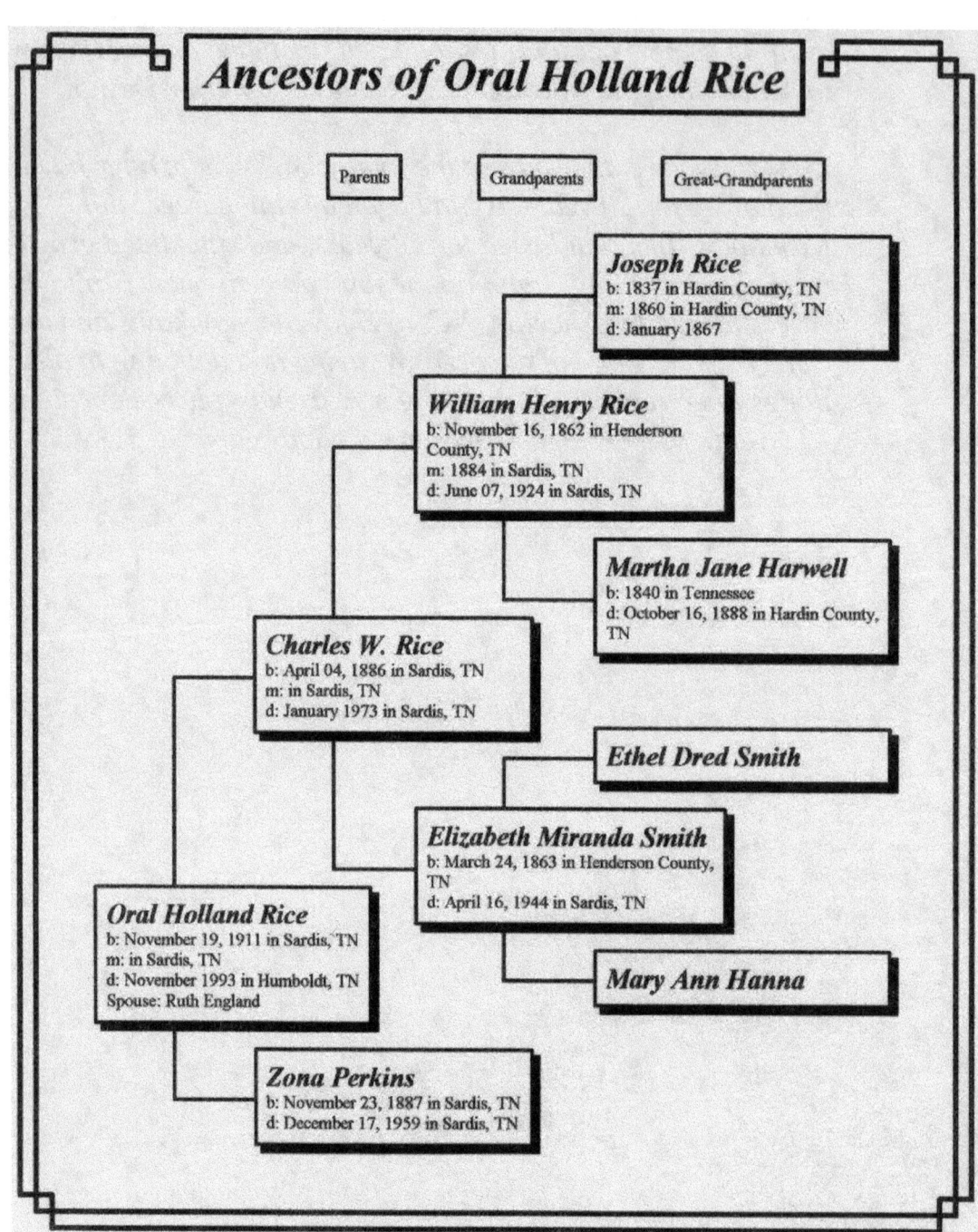

Joseph Rice
b: 1837 in Hardin County, TN
m: 1860 in Hardin County, TN
d: January 1867

William Henry Rice
b: November 16, 1862 in Henderson County, TN
m: 1884 in Sardis, TN
d: June 07, 1924 in Sardis, TN

Martha Jane Harwell
b: 1840 in Tennessee
d: October 16, 1888 in Hardin County, TN

Charles W. Rice
b: April 04, 1886 in Sardis, TN
m: in Sardis, TN
d: January 1973 in Sardis, TN

Ethel Dred Smith

Elizabeth Miranda Smith
b: March 24, 1863 in Henderson County, TN
d: April 16, 1944 in Sardis, TN

Oral Holland Rice
b: November 19, 1911 in Sardis, TN
m: in Sardis, TN
d: November 1993 in Humboldt, TN
Spouse: Ruth England

Mary Ann Hanna

Zona Perkins
b: November 23, 1887 in Sardis, TN
d: December 17, 1959 in Sardis, TN

GENERATION THREE

Holland Oral Rice married Ruth England
DOB: 11-19-1911 DOD: 11-1993
Ruth England DOB: 01-28-1918 DOD: 09-22-1978

My grandfather was Holland Oral Rice and he was married to Ruth England Rice.

Their Children: Since these individuals are still living, I am not posting much information about them.

    Margaret Anita Rice
    Linda Jane Rice
    Mickey Dianne Rice

Ruth England Rice and Holland Rice

Holland Rice – age 19

Ruth England Rice and Holland Rice

My cousins and I knew that our grandfather, Holland was a wonderful man and we called him "grin-daddy". He loved his children and grandchildren and we all have many happy memories of being with him. He was a wonderful grandfather to all of us. I remember he had albino white squirrels in his yard in Jackson, TN and had trained them to eat out of his hand. We always played games when we visited and he would cook us fun meals. We would ride around with him in his car to do errands. He had a hug and a smile for all of us.

Holland grew up in Sardis and did many different jobs during his life. He was the Assistant Postmaster in Savannah, TN and also had side jobs with the railroad and drug store. He is best known for helping others and changing the lives of many friends and family members. He lived in Savannah for many years, Sardis, TN, Jackson, TN and Humboldt, TN. He died of Parkinson's disease at age 84.

Ruth England's parents were James England and Mary McKinney also from Sardis, TN.

My Aunt Mickey describes her memories of her parents, Holland and Ruth Rice.

"Daddy (Holland), Lucy, Paul and Cecil reached adulthood, but they had two brothers (Howard and the other name escapes me and one sister (Mildred) who died at ten months old with dysentery. Howard was two years older than Daddy and died of a ruptured appendix at twelve years of age. They couldn't operate for that at that time and they just sent him home to die. Daddy sat by his bed with him until he died which took about three days. Daddy cried every time I asked him about it.

Everyone always loved Daddy (Holland) and there is no telling how many folks he helped to get a job. There just weren't any jobs in Sardis unless you farmed or owned the General Store.

Daddy died at 84 and he was buried in Sardis. The day of his funeral it was pouring down rain. However, the little Sardis Methodist Church was full and I was shocked because usually by then all of your friends are either dead or in bad health and don't make it to your funeral. I (for the most part) only knew family members so I went around greeting everyone and thanked them for coming. In one way or another, they all said, "I would have come today no matter what the weather was because your Daddy and Mother let me live with in Memphis until he found me a job in Memphis and I got on my feet. I don't know what I would have done without his help." That was "soo" Daddy! - always helping someone.

And mother (Ruth) nearly worked herself to death waiting on everyone and cooking delicious meals. She had her flowers growing in every conceivable place so we always had fresh flowers in the middle of the Dining Room table unless it was the dead of winter. We just had two bedrooms and one bath (which was normal then), but mother had made a beautiful floral cover for the roll-away bed which was kept in the Sun Parlor along with the piano, telephone table and a large chair and that parlor was used as a bedroom too as often as not.

She also was the nurse and the parlor was the hospital room when anybody in the family had surgery in Memphis until they were able to make the trip home. It just seemed normal to me that we had company all the time.

And I just don't ever remember Daddy saying he was tired! He had more energy than ten people. He had his Rural postal Route. Then you could go into work as early as you wanted because the mail was coming into the post office every few hours day and night. So he would get up at 4:30 then be home from his route by about 10:00 A.M. so he could work a shift on the railroad that afternoon when they needed him. He also worked at a Drug Store downtown at night some times. And he sold cars. He also sold Real Estate and kept his listings by the phone and taught us *girls how to look up any questions about houses for sale if someone called when he was gone to another job. He juggled all these jobs. And every time you turned around he had bought a new car to surprise mother. I bet it was sure a surprise all right! But they absolutely "adored" each other and she would run out of the house to see it and we'd all jump in the car to go for a ride. They never argued in front of us. I always just knew something wasn't right if she said "come on, we're going on to Sardis ourselves". When you asked if Daddy was coming, she'd say "Don't worry, he'll be there". And he would be within hours.*

Daddy was always playing with politics! He took me everywhere with him when he was off work and he'd stop by to see whoever and they'd give me an ice cream cone or something. He seemed to know everyone in the world. I was so proud of him! All of my girlfriends in elementary school in Memphis just loved him and would run up and hug him just like they would their own father.

After supper every night (this was before TVs) he'd ask Anita, Linda and me what we wanted to play. Listen to a mystery on the radio, monopoly, cards, etc. He had as much fun as we did. He always played the games with us. And he never left me out even though I was the youngest. He would just help me if I couldn't read something, etc. He had the patience of JOB. He helped us with our homework and always thought everything we did was wonderful. It was like being raised by your grandfather he was so lenient.

He was a Shriner so we got to go to the Shriner Circus several times every year. Linda and I both fell in love with the Lion Trainer and planned to marry him some day.

Then when a friend surprised Anita with a little black puppy, she smiled and said "thank you" and as soon as he drove off, she turned around to me and said "Do you want a puppy?" I was out of my mind. It turned out it wasn't just a cocker spaniel, it was also had chow. So after it started tearing the clothes off the line and biting everybody but me, Mother sent

Daddy to have birds and bees talk with me. Something like this: Mickey, it is time for Blackie to get married and there aren't any dogs on this street he wants to marry so I'm going to take him to Savannah where there are a lot of dogs for him to choose from and they can have a lot of puppies and be free to run and play. They don't have any rules about dogs in Savannah like they do in Memphis. It broke my heart, but he assured me every time he went to Savannah to check on Grandmother and Granddaddy that he saw my dog running all over town with his friends. And that he just loved it!!!

By the way, Daddy was Assistant Postmaster in Savannah. Tom Murray (Congressman) created the job for Daddy so we could move to Savannah for him to take care of Grandmother. Then after we sisters grew up, Daddy and Mother moved back to Memphis and Daddy went to work at the Regional Post Office Headquarters that over the 11 southern states. He retired from there several years later.

Also, another memory. When we were growing up in Memphis, Mother belonged to the Eastern Stars (I think the female version of the Shiners). We loved for her to go to her meetings (I guess monthly) because Daddy babysat us. What a joke! We weren't allowed to EVER wear our evening dresses mother had made us to wear in our piano recitals - EVER! - unless Daddy was in charge! We whispered all day about what we were going to do as soon as mother left. Mother and Daddy always acted like they didn't know. We would get those long dresses out, paint our nails RED, put on mother's red EARSCREWS (they called them that then) and put on music and dance and turn flips all over the house for hours until we knew it was time for mother to come home. Daddy would hide behind his newspaper and laugh till tears ran down his face watching us. We were all going to be movie stars, of course! No problem! What else!!

What can I say? We were just beautiful!!!!!! When anyone told our parents that they had such beautiful daughters, we knew it was the TRUTH! Cause Daddy had already told us. I could go on forever I have so many wonderful childhood memories, but just suffice it to say, It rocked!!!! I know one thing - I still can't believe how lucky I was to have parents like they were. So happy and so much fun!! I remember having my playhouse at both my grandparents homes and also in our Memphis yard. I especially loved the one in Savannah because I got to use Granddaddy's sawdust for topping for my mud pies and cakes. In Memphis, Linda taught me how to decorate them with mother's flowers. And in Savannah, Granddaddy Rice (Charles Walter) would plant a baby garden for me at the end of his big people garden!! And Sardis was special because all my cousins on mother's side were there and we had a blast!"

Another one about Daddy. Mother used to have a black woman named "Fannie" who came to iron one day a week for us in Memphis when I was little. We all adored her! She and her husband had six children. One day I was just waking up from my nap and Daddy came to sit on my bed after taking Fannie home. He had tears in his eyes and said that when he took her home, her husband was waiting for her at the door and told her he had lost his job. Daddy said they were so devastated because it was the first part of December and they had no idea where they might get the money for Santa to come at Christmas.

So since I was getting to be a "big girl", he was wondering if since I had 3 dolls and 3 big stuffed animals, I'd want to let Fannie and her husband have them to give their children for Christmas. To be perfectly honest, I was really bonded with my dolls and animals so it wasn't the best idea I'd ever heard; however, neither could I imagine what it would feel like to get up on Christmas morning and have nothing under the tree!??! So naturally I said yes and he took me with him to their home. I'll never forget it. When we walked into their home, it was spotless, Fannie was peeling potatoes in the kitchen preparing supper and her husband sitting at the breakfast room table reading the Bible out loud to both of them. They just lit up when we walked in and when Daddy showed them what we had brought, I'll remember the looks on their faces as long as I live. It made my heart change forever to see how something I took for granted could be "everything" to six little children at Christmas. It seemed like back then everyone had time to be nicer and more compassionate with each other.

And when anyone on our street was sick or had a death in their family, Mother could always stretch whatever she had cooked for me to take a plate to their door. I just loved to do that so if I ask and she didn't have enough till the next day or something, I'd run out to my playhouse in the backyard and make them a mud pie, decorate it and deliver it and tell them we were so sorry. We always had flowers for me to take from Mother's flower beds and if ours weren't blooming at that time, then the man next door would give me some of his. Any good that is in me came from just watching how they treated others and I am so thankful.

Another wonderful quality of my parents was their advice. There was no problem they couldn't solve with some sage cliche that had been passed down for generations. (I know that from listening to the adults in Sardis talking around the fireplace when I was suppose to be asleep.)

For instance, when someone insulted or infuriated me, and I had no idea how to respond but felt if I didn't ulcers were on the way, Daddy would say " ignore it, it is better to have the good will of a dog than the bad". Mother would say, 'CONSIDER THE SOURCE"! I would have told THEM - "YADA, YADA". So I realized later in life (in a self-analytic moment) that I do both. I tell them what I think, then I ignore the situation. It works for me. That way, we all get to share the ulcers."

My Aunt Linda Rice tells of her memories of her parents, Holland and Ruth.

"I remember hours and hours of hearing the sewing machine running. Mother made us beautiful clothes (sometimes matching), particularly for special occasions. The one that sticks in my mind was a beautiful long dress of aqua chintz with ruffles to the floor that she stitched up for a piano recital! And each Easter, we had magnificent

homemade corsages fashioned of flowers from her prolific garden---gardenias, daisies, sweet peas---whatever was in bloom. "Store-bought" carnations (usually worn by our classmates) were too pricey for our family, so Mother always made do with what she had.

Dinner (almost every single night!) was in the dining room with an ironed white tablecloth and home-cooked food. Pork chops, mashed potatoes with English peas (we called them a "bird nest" because the peas were placed in the center of a dollop of potatoes like a nest of bird eggs). Her special "candle salad" consisted of a slice of pineapple with half a peeled banana standing in the center as the "candle". Mayonnaise formed the drip of "tallow" and a cherry represented the fire on top. I can still taste it.

I can also remember as a preschooler that each afternoon after naptime, we were cleaned up, brushed up, and spotless (Mother too) for Daddy's arrival home from work.

He would also tame the squirrels in his yard and had incredible patience. and the squirrels eventually came to regard him as their *daddy as well as ours!*

My one-on-one time with Daddy was often in a fishing boat. When we went to Sardis and Savannah on the weekends, I would sometimes elect to be in Savannah with Daddy while Anita and Mickey went to Sardis. We got in an old wooden fishing boat and anchored under the Tennessee River bridge at Savannah. I don't think I ever caught a fish, so Daddy would let me collect mussel shells on the river bank before we left to go home (so I wouldn't be completely empty-handed!).

Another vivid memory was Daddy as a true political animal. *Once he took me with him to the palatial home of E. H. Crump (the famous "Boss Crump" of Memphis) and I stood goggle-eyed as he talked to Mr. Crump on behalf of one of his friends about some sort of political appointment. In those days, everything was tied to the "patronage* system" which declared that whoever was in political power had the right to get jobs for their cronies. Daddy loved being the advocate for the down-and-out and would go to any lengths to get them the favors he thought they deserved. Every time I pass the old Crump home here in Memphis, I remember my astonishment when a butler answered the door and ushered us inside. I had never seen anything so grand---especially when Mr. Crump descended that huge staircase in his dapper clothes--- polished cane in hand.

On the eve of the Truman/Dewey presidential election (1948, I think, when I was 8 years old) I stayed up ALL NIGHT with Daddy in front of the old upright radio and posted the latest numbers on a piece of poster board, which he had divided into 48 columns to keep track of the state totals. He called out the numbers and I posted them on the poster chart. Dewey (a Republican) was supposed to be a sure-fire winner, but Daddy (a yellow-dog Democrat through and through) wouldn't go to bed and give up. So neither would I, though my eyes got so heavy I thought I was going to pass out. When Truman pulled ahead in the wee hours of the morning, Daddy was ecstatic!

On his rural mail route, I sometimes got to be an unofficial assistant when the VERY heavy Sears Catalogs came in and had to be delivered by the hundreds. He let me skip school and hide on the floorboard of the back seat (child labor laws and all that - ha!). When we got out of town (and away from the probing eyes of the postal officials) I would scramble up and help him stuff a huge catalog in every mailbox. The colorful catalogs were considered treasures back then (not just for ordering everything under the sun, but eventually as substitute toilet paper for some folks,) and sometimes the recipients would be waiting on their porches for the sight of his car."

My mother Anita Rice Fletcher shares her memories of her parents Holland and Ruth Rice.

"After they bought the house at 514 E. Davant in Memphis, Mother was happier (I think) than she'd ever been because they finally owned rather than rented and she felt she could settle down. She loved to raise flowers and always had gardenia bushes, as well as snowball bushes (I can't remember their real name). Dinner together was a family affair every night, white tablecloth on the DR table, and Daddy laughing and talking with us. Mother was a good cook and really knew how to flavor dishes. She didn't actually require much help from us girls in terms of the cooking itself, but we set the table and did the dishes and whatever was asked of us. Keeping house and taking care of the family was her life, rather than having much of a social life. The house was always clean, smelled good, with fresh flowers around.

I would ride my bicycle to the neighborhood grocery store to get Mother's grocery list filled, and just sign the bill. She was always very specific about cuts of meat and brands of canned goods. The grocer held accounts for his customers and billed us monthly, as I recall. Eddie was his name and he was an expert "meat man". Later we discovered he also was a talented singer who performed in Memphis.

Mickey or Linda wrote about Daddy's multiple jobs, and I remember it that way, too. He enjoyed his jobs because he was such an extrovert, loved interacting with people, and had lots of energy. We used to go visit him at the drugstore where he worked nights, and he'd give us chewing gum and Hershey bars. He took delight always in introducing Mother and us girls to his co-workers.

My overall childhood memories are of a happy home and of parents who loved us unconditionally.

When Mother would get peeved with Daddy over something, he never seemed to react badly. He would just grin and tease her and they'd make up. Years later when Mother was in bed so much (back trouble) he would wait on her hand and foot, going out to get meals for them."

GENERATION FOUR

Charles Rice and Zona Perkins
Charles DOB: 04-04-1886   DOD: 01-1973
 Zona Perkins: DOB: 11-23-1887   DOD: 12-17-1959

Their Children:
> **Oral Holland (1911-1993) married Ruth England**
> Rupard Kerry Rice (1913-),
> Howard (-1918) – ruptured appendix at age 12
> Charles Cecil Rice (1917-1991) married Evelyn Welch
> Mildred Rice (1919-1919), died of dysentery at age ten months
> Paul (1921-1991) married Mildred Martin. He was in the army
> Millie Lucille Rice (1925-) married Paul Martin

My great grandparents were Charles Rice and Zona Perkins.
 I do have early memories of my great granddaddy.   We visited him in Sardis when we were younger and ate watermelon at a picnic table. Charles was a great carpenter and he and Zona ran the phone office for many years.   They lived a peaceful, simple life in Sardis, TN.   Zona Perkins's parents were Mack and Liddie Perkins.

   My aunt Linda describes memories of her grandparents Charles Walter and Zona.

"Gr. Rice let me play in his carpentry shop. He nailed a 12-in. stick onto a small wooden "circle", and we used it for a pretend microphone. Many "radio shows" and stellar performances on those wooden mikes."

My Aunt Mickey describes her memories of Charles Walter.

"When I was little and went to Savannah w/Daddy to spend the weekend with Granddaddy (Charles Walter Rice). I stayed in his shop with him a lot while he did carpentry work and that is why I always thought he was a carpenter; however, I discovered when we moved back to Savannah when I was twelve that he had retired from being Manager of the Sardis Telephone Company. No one had ever mentioned it until some ladies at First Methodist Church in Savannah told me that and how they had loved my grandmother (Zona Perkins Rice) who had always helped him at the telephone company. (I guess a woman before her time!)

Granddaddy (Charles Walter) always patted me on the back and told me I was a "Dandy!" And I would get up to have coffee with him at 4:30 A.M. each morning and we'd put our feel on the big stove in the middle of the house that heated the whole house and I'd snuggle up to him while he read his Bible. When he died, his Bibles were well-worn and had many things underlines, and notes in the margins, etc."

My mother, Anita Rice Fletcher tells of her memories of Charles Walter and Zona Perkins.

"Most of my memories of Zona, my grandmother, are of her being in bed most all the time, in the house they rented on Pickwick Street in Savannah. She was sweet but quite sick for several years. My cousin Joanne, who was a nurse, surmised that it was pellegra , which was a vitamin-deficiency disease most often found in sailors at sea. Before Zona got so sick, I remember her boiling the laundry in big black iron tubs in the back yard. Yes, boiling water. And poking the clothes around with a long stick, lifting them into rinsing water, then hanging all of it on a clothesline.

Aunt Lucille had moved in with them to help take care of them. She had a full-time job as well. I loved to go visit them so I could hang out with Lucille and her girlfriends (they were a hoot and very much o.k. with a child as extra baggage). I got to play in Granddaddy Rice's (Walter) workshop. He was easy-going and so generous with his supplies and his time. He had the patience of Job. I built a little telephone with the parts and pieces of wood, then set out a "house" in the dirt area in the back yard. The "house" consisted of the outline of rooms with yet more wood pieces.

After Zona died and Lucille married Paul Martin (Corky), they moved Granddaddy into a nice trailer in their own yard in Counce, TN. Lucy cooked for all of them and took care of his needs. He was alert, agile and healthy (as far as I know) for years and seemed happy with his situation.

From the website Tennessee Yesteryears and the History of Sardis by David Donahue and Brenda Fiddler. There is an excerpt about Charles Walter and Zona Rice and the telephone company.

"We aren't sure when the first telephone system came to Sardis but we think it was around 1905. The first one was very primitive and you were only sure of service when the weather was clear. There were only party lines and there were usually ten or more families on each line. No message was ever private for, when the phone rang for anyone, it rang in every house on that line. Each family was assigned his own combination of long and short rings which was equivalent to our phone numbers today. You were only supposed to listen when it was your number of rings. But that ringing phone exerted a powerful influence on those people who were near the phone and, consequently, almost every phone receiver was picked up so that one might learn the news. If you were outside and heard your phone and failed to reach it in time, you could ring once, get the operator and find out who had just called -- almost like having an answering service. The first telephone office was near where the Methodist Church is now located. During the next few years, it was located at two other sites in town. It was in buildings that *had an upstairs, once where Billy Duck's insurance office is located, and the other where L & W Grocery now stands. As far as we were able to discover, among the first telephone systems, was a stock company known as Center Point Telephone Company with Walter Rice as manager. Some of the ladies who served as telephone operators were Misses Tola and Sarah Davey, Ora Ellis, Millie Wheatley, Lee Piercy Stanfill, Bertie Presley Hanna, Lorena Holland, Kayte Holland, and Mattie Moffit Ford.*

Mr. Rice assumed control of the company about 1930 and he and his family ran the office until the mid-1940s, when Mr. and Mrs. Ray Little took it over. In 1951, a stockholder company was formed known as Sardis Telephone Company. A new switchboard was purchased, new lines were built and many new phones were installed. Les Huff was appointed to be the manager. This system provided satisfactory service until Tennessee Telephone Company purchased the Sardis system, for one dollar, and assumed control in 1958."

Charles Walter Rice

Charles Walter Rice

Charles Walter Rice and Zona Perkins Rice

Zona Perkins Rice with her sons, left to right Kerry, Zona, Holland, Cecil and baby Paul

Zona and Charles with Paul (army) on the right and ____ on the left

Charles Walter Rice and daughter Lucille

Zona Perkins Rice

The Rice Boys. Left to right Kerry, Cecil and Holland Rice

The Rice Boys: left to right Holland, Neal, Cecil, Paul

1951 Sardis left to right: Neal Rice, Jenny Grissom,
Cecil Rice, Lucille Rice, Holland Rice and Marie Ellis

Charles Walter Rice with great grandchildren Suzanne and Katherine
Fletcher.

Charles Walter and Zona Rice gravestone.
Spring Hill Cemetery, Sardis, TN

* also from Tnyesteryear.com and the History of Sardis, TN

The nation needed more men for every area of service. They quickly set up machinery to register young men. At first only the single men and men without children were drafted into service. Among those who served from Sardis and surrounding area were Herman Lane, R. C. Hopper, Elbert Hanna, Clif Bingham, **Tom Grissom**, Harrison Shirley, Newt Adams, **Eather Rice**, Grover Wiley, Leo Presley, Tom Phillips, Robert Hodgins, Elbert Grissom, Cal Bivens, Hobart Craig, Elbert Weaver, Ily Everett, Fred Wilhite, R. C. McMurray, Frank Presley, Ophia Holland, Claude Montgomery, **William Homer Rice**, Elmer Phillips, Elbert Bivens, Jet Smith, and Clarence Hanna. Among those who gave their lives in service to our country were Elmer Phillips, Claud Montgomery, Elbert Bivens and Lynn McNatt.

GENERATION FIVE

William Henry Rice and Elizabeth Miranda Smith
DOB: 11-16-1862 DOD: 06-07-1924 Sardis, TN

Miranda: DOB: 03-24-1863 DOD: 04-16-1944 Sardis, TN
Miranda's parents were Ethel Dred Smith and Mary Hanna

Their Children:

James Eather (1888-1967) married Grace Louette
    Phillips

Charles Walter – (1885-1973) married Zona Perkins

Mae (Mary) Jane (1889-1978) married Thomas Kirk
    Mae supposedly dated Tom Grissom for years but she
    married Thomas J. Kirk. The Rice's and Grissom's lived ½
    mile from each other and were close friends. Mae attended
    grammar school and high school and taught school. She
    moved many times because she didn't like staying in one
    place. She always lived close by her parents. She hated
    housework but was an excellent seamstress who made all
    her own clothes.

William Homer (1894-1933) married Mary Moffett
    Served in WW I

Madison Escart. (1891-1931) married Jimmie Petty

Ora Anne (1894-1911) died at age 17 of typhoid

Thomas Wesley – (1900-1901) died age 1 of typhoid

Hattie Emma (1899-1993) married Robert Elmer
    Grissom. She finished high school and lived with Charles
    Walter and Zona Perkins. She helped them with being the
    telephone operator. She left Sardis when her true love,
    Robert Elmer Grissom returned from France after the war.
    She got married in the Rice house in Hinkle. She lived in
    Sardis for a while as her husband was the principal at the
    Wake Forest School and also was a teacher. They left for
    Oklahoma to accept a job as a school principal near
    Okemah where they permanently settled. Robert Grissom
    had lived in Oklahoma before the war and was a
    bookkeeper in his cousin's business. She died in Texas

William Henry Rice and wife Elizabeth Miranda Smith
Children: left to right Madison Escart, James Eather, Charles Walter,
(Mary) Mae, William Homer and baby Hattie Emma. Taken in 1899

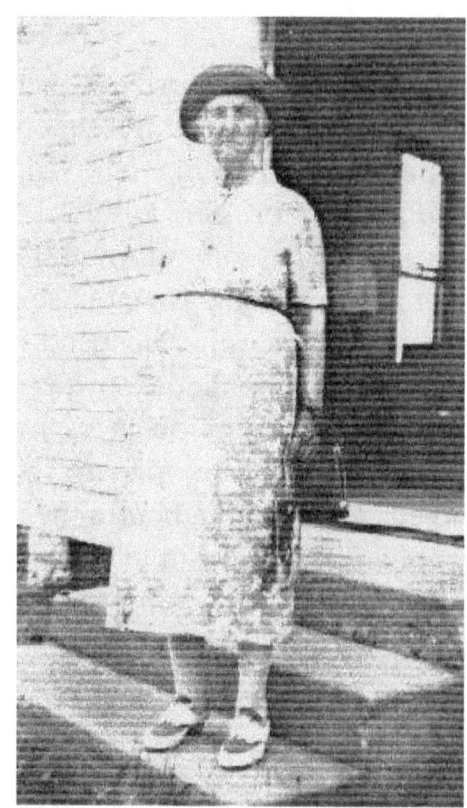

Elizabeth Miranda Smith Rice "called Grandma Mindy"

Ora Anne Rice who died at 17 of typhoid

Emma, Eather and Mae Rice (siblings)

William married Elizabeth Miranda Smith in Sardis, TN
He taught penmanship for many years. He was
reportedly quiet, kind and never talked much. He died of a non-
healing sore on his shoulder blade (which we know think was
cancer). After William's death, Elizabeth went to live with Mae
and TJ in Sardis. She was a very strong woman and made three
trips to Oklahoma to see her daughters. One of these trips was her
first train ride. She stayed three months on her first visit but drove
Mae crazy. She died at Mae's house in 1944.

Grave of William Henry and Miranda Rice
Spring Hill Cemetery, Sardis, TN

Ancestors of Joseph Rice

| Parents | Grandparents | Great-Grandparents |

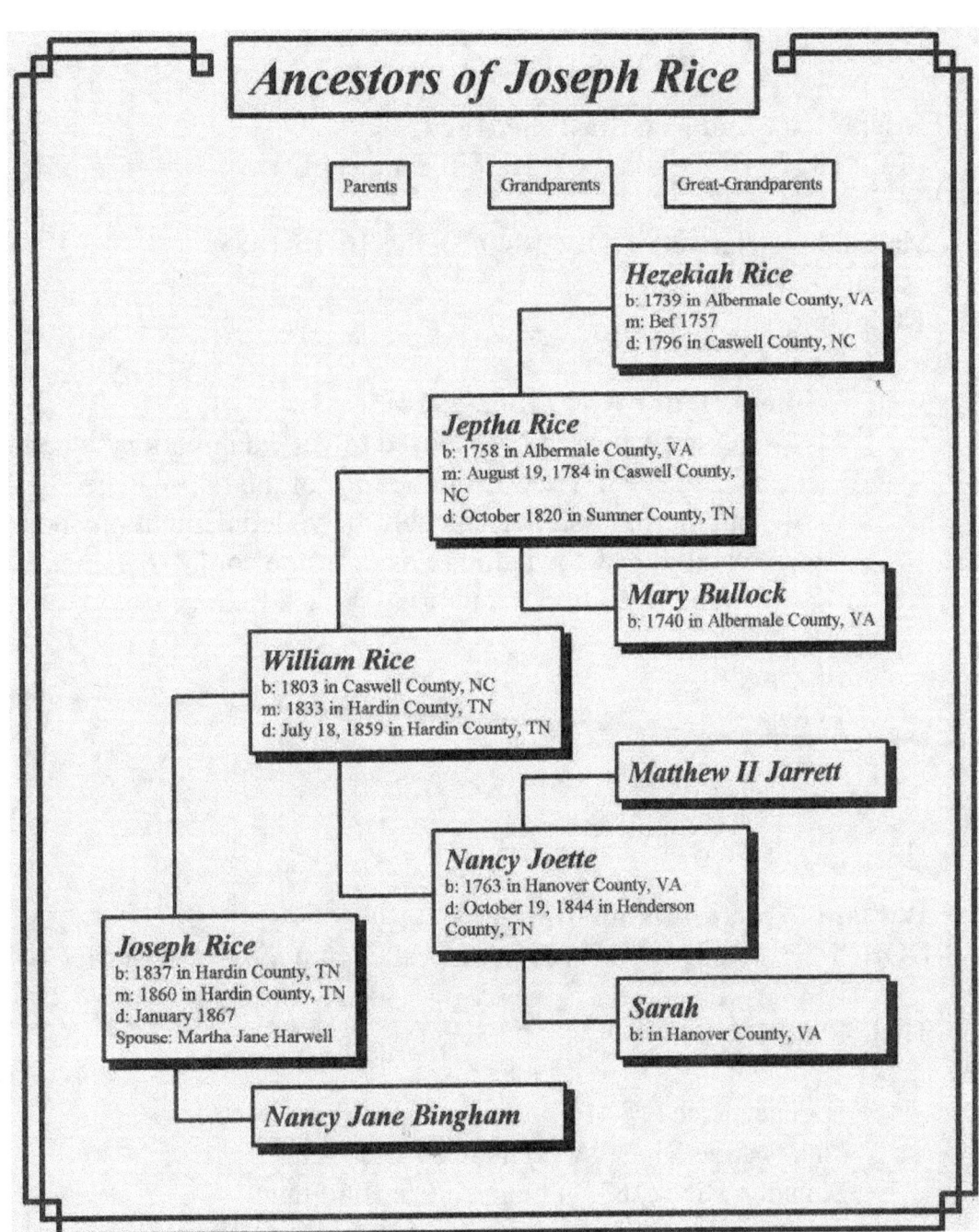

Hezekiah Rice
b: 1739 in Albermale County, VA
m: Bef 1757
d: 1796 in Caswell County, NC

Jeptha Rice
b: 1758 in Albermale County, VA
m: August 19, 1784 in Caswell County, NC
d: October 1820 in Sumner County, TN

Mary Bullock
b: 1740 in Albermale County, VA

William Rice
b: 1803 in Caswell County, NC
m: 1833 in Hardin County, TN
d: July 18, 1859 in Hardin County, TN

Matthew II Jarrett

Nancy Joette
b: 1763 in Hanover County, VA
d: October 19, 1844 in Henderson County, TN

Joseph Rice
b: 1837 in Hardin County, TN
m: 1860 in Hardin County, TN
d: January 1867
Spouse: Martha Jane Harwell

Sarah
b: in Hanover County, VA

Nancy Jane Bingham

GENERATION SIX

Joseph Rice and Martha Jane Harwell
DOB: 1837 DOD: 01-1867 Hardin County, TN

Martha Jane Harwell DOB: 1840 DOD: 10-16-1888

Their children:

William Henry Rice (1862-1924)
He rarely cussed but he used to yell "damnation" when it was needed. He was on the roof of the house once hammering and hurt himself, he yelled damnation and would throw the hammer as far as he could, then make someone go find it and bring it back to him.
Axey
Elizabeth
Louisa

GENERATION SEVEN

William Rice and Nancy Bingham
DOB: 1803 DOD: 07-18-1859 Caswell County, NC to Hardin Co, TN

Their Children:

Barbary Rice (1834)
Nancy Jane Rice (1833) married Burl Pitts
Amanda Rice (1835-) married Charlie Flatt
Joseph Rice (1837-) married Martha Jane Harwell
Joseph was a Captain in the 29th infantry in the Civil war. He served 1861-1863 on the Union side of the army. Most of Hardin County, TN was Union.

Elizabeth Rice (1839) married Alfred Pitts
Adelaide Rice married P.H. Stevens
Wesley Alexander Rice married Ducie Caroline Hopper

GENERATION EIGHT

Jeptha Rice and Nancy Joette
DOB: 1758 DOD: 10-1820

Nancy Joette DOB: 1763 Hanover Co, VA DOD: 10-19-1844
Albermarle County, VA to Caswell Co, NC to Sumner Co, TN
Nancy's parents are Matthew Harris Joette and Margaret Henderson
Allen.

Their Children:

> P. Kensas (1798-1826) married Mary Polly Pond
> Mary Polly Rice (1788-1847) married Lepaton L.
>   Iverson and Levi Smith (died in Hardin Co TN)
> Matthew Rice (1800-1823) married Sarah Sally Pond
> Elizabeth Rice (1796-1853) married William Posea
> Baldwin Rice (1795-)
> Martha Patsey Rice (1805-1866) married Elisha Gibson
> Axey Rice (1805-1859) married Henry Perry Smith
> **William Rice (1803-1859) married Nancy Jane Bingham**
> Joseph Henry Rice (1803-1859) married Melissa Ambrose
> > It appears Joseph Rice served in the Civil War. His wife
> > Martha, remarried in 1868 to Loftin King Delaney. She
> > died of Tuberculosis at age 48. They began in Sumner Co,
> > TN and died in Caldwell, Texas.

Jeptha Rice received a land grant from his service in the war in 1821.
He received 2500 acres in the State of Tennessee, Hardin County. He
left this land to several of his relatives to be split up.

Jeptha, the son of Hezekiah and Mary was born in Albermarle County, VA. He married August 19, 1784 in Caswell County, NC to Nancy Joette. Her parents were Matthew II and Sarah Joette of Hanover County, VA and Caswell County, NC.

In Caswell Co, NC, Jeptha enlisted in the Revolutionary War for the duration of seven years on March 15, 1777. He served as a private, Ensign, Quartermaster Sargent and a first Lieutenant. He was wounded across the chest by a bayonet and not mustered from January 1778 to May 1781 when he reenlisted on May 15, 17781. *This information was obtained by war records and Nancy's deposition for his pension.

Three of the sons also served in wars. A land warrant was due to Jeptha but the army thought he had no heirs. The warrant was claimed by Church Rice, son of Gideon Rice. Jeptha's family went to court to establish their heirship in order to receive Jeptha's land warrant. In 1827 the family was recognized as the true heirs and a land warrant for 2560 acres was issued. The land was later divided among many family members and was located in the northwest of Hardin County and into McNairy County, TN.

JEPTHA RICE LAND GRANT – Recorded October 12, 1827

TO ALL TO WHOM THESE PRESENTS SHALL COME --- GREETINGS:

KNOW YE that in consideration of Military Service performed by Jeptha Rice to the state of North Carolina Warrant No. 958 dated the 6 day of September 1821 for 2560 acres and entered on the 3rd day of April 1823 by No. 1235.

There is granted by the said State of Tennessee, unto Baldwin Rice, Levi Smith & Polly his wife, Kenas Rice, William Posea & Elizabeth his wife, Matthew Rice, Elisha Gibson & Patsy his wife, Joseph Rice, _____ Smith & Axey his wife, & Henry Rice heirs of the said Jeptha Rice, dec'd.

A certain tract or parcel of Land, containing twenty five hundred & sixty acres by survey bearing the date 15 day of August 1823, lying in the ninth district in Hardin County in ranges 5 & 6 & sections five and six and bounded as follows, to wit: Beginning in Section 5th & range 5th at a stake the southwest corner of Entry No. 1082. Thence East with its line fifty poles to an ironwood the south east corner of the same, thence north twenty-five poles to a stake its north east corner on the south boundary of entry No. 181 & crossing Doe River at 3 poles, thence east with the line of entry No 181 fifty-six poles to a dogwood, its south east corner. Thence North 140 poles to a double poplar its corner on the range line, thence West 80 poles to a hickory its corner, thence North 300 poles to a black oak. Thence East 370 poles to a spanish oak, sweet gum and ironwood. Thence South 440 poles to a hickory on the North Boundary of entry No. 1175. Thence West 130 poles to a stake on the east boundary of entry No. 1093. Thence North one hundred poles to a stake, its north east corner, thence west 88 poles to a hickory its north west corner, thence south 350 poles to two maples on the north boundary or entry No. 1834. Thence West two hundred & twenty poles to a black oak its north west corner, thence south 265 poles to a hickory, thence west 443 poles to a post oak, thence north 490 poles to a hickory Thence east four hundred and eighty five poles to the beginning.

With the hereintaments (?) and appertenances. TO HAVE AND TO HOLD the said tract or parcel of land with its appertenances to the said heirs of Jeptha Rice, Dec'd, as above named, and their heirs forever. In witness whereof William Carroll, Governor of the State of Tennessee, hath hereunto set his hand, and caused the great seal of the state to be affixed, at Nashville on the 29 day of June in the year of our Lord one thousand eight hundred and twenty-seven and of the independence of the United States the 51st.

(Signed)   of the Govenor: Wm.Carroll

Daniel Graham, Secretary

TRANSCRIBED -

Jeptha and Nancy migrated to Sumner County, TN between 1801 and 1811.   Jeptha is listed as a Davidson County resident in 1812 and was a member of Captain McAdams Davidson County Militia in 1811. An affidavit made by John Clark in 1839 says that the Rices moved to Sumner County, TN around 1800 settling on Mansker's Creek (dividing line between Davidson and Sumner County).   A few years later they moved to Shane's Creek where they lived until Jeptha's death.

According to the medical doctors record, he made eight visits to Jeptha during his illness beginning October 1, 1817. His wife, Nancy was the administrator of the estate. Jeptha was buried in Hendersonville, TN maybe the Gibson Family Cemetery.

Nancy Jouett is the daughter of Matthew Harris Jouett and Margaret Henderson Allen. She was born 1763 in Caswell, North Carolina, USA. Her father was Matthew Jouett II was a prominent Colonial Settler of Caswell County, North Carolina, coming there when it was still part of Orange County. He was the son of Matthew Jouett I and Susanna Moore (or Price) Jouett of Hanover, Louisa and Albermarle Counties, Virginia - - being of Huguenot ancestry.

Nancy's father, Matthew Jouett II was a Soldier in the French and Indian War. He was from an old and influential family of Virginia, he was prominent in the affairs of Louisa County as was his father before him.

Nancy died on 19 Oct 1844 in Sumner County, Tennessee.
They were married on 19 Aug 1784 in Caswell, North Carolina, USA. They had 8 children.

Here is a deposition in Nancy's own words about her husband Jeptha Rice.

Pension Application Of Jeptha Rice, Natl Archives Microseries M804, Roll 2032, Application #W5700 Carteret County, North Carolina, August 23rd, 1821

Sumner County, Tennessee, October 14th, 1838, personally appeared, Nancy Rice, aged 76 years:

"That they were married a short time before the surrender of Lord Cornwallis. Her said husband, the said Jeptha Rice entered Revolutionary service as well as she remembers, either in the company commanded by his father, Hezekiah Rice or the company commanded by Captain Winn Dickson [or Dixon] and was attached to the regiment commanded by Colonel Henry Dixon of the North Carolina line. Her said husband enlisted for three years or during the war. Soon after he entered the service he was promoted to the rank of first lieutenant, which grade he held until about the close of his service she was informed he took the rank of captain..." "Her said husband was taken sick and was furloughed and came home. While on this visit home, he and declarant intermarried before his term of service expired. After their marriage which was as before stated as well as she can remember, was on the 27th day of August 1781. After her marriage, her said husband went on one tour of duty to the army and after his return home he held himself in constant readiness to return to the army whenever called on until the whole Revolutionary soldiers were disbanded."

"Her husband, the said Jeptha Rice, performed much hard service in the Revolutionary War. He was in the Battle of Eutaw Springs, in Gates' Defeat, in the Battle of Guilford and several other engagements. She thinks he was in the battle of Brandywine and Monmouth. The last two battles she has not so distinct a recollection as the other three engagements before named. She remember however to have heard him often speak of being engaged in a severe engagement which was fought on a Monday when many of the soldiers were overcome by the severe heat and while in this condition drank free of cold water from which several of them died, and she thinks this battle of which her husband spoke was the Battle of Brandywine, but in this however, she may be mistaken. In one of the engagements he was wounded in the fleshy part of his breast, the scar of which was visible to the day of his death."

Here is the deposition from Joseph H. Rice, Jeptha's son in 1853:

Davidson County, Tennessee, June 14th, 1853, Joseph H. Rice aged 49 years, personally appeared: "That he is the son and administrator of the said Nancy Rice, who was a Revolutionary pensioner of the United States…That he has often heard his father, the said Jeptha Rice, speak of his services in the Revolutionary War. That at the beginning of the war, he was living in Caswell County in the state of North Carolina, and that he entered the service in said county and state in the company commanded by his father Hezekiah Rice. This was at the commencement of hostilities in North Carolina. This service was performed as a private, as declarant thinks." "That sometime subsequent to his first enlistment, to wit, in or about the year 1776, as declarant thinks, his father was promoted to ensign, and soon thereafter to lieutenant in the regiment commanded by Lt. Colonel Henry Dixon, who had been promoted from captain. That his father continued to serve as a lieutenant in said regiment for several years. That after his father's death, to wit, in the year 1825, a suit was brought by the heirs of his father, the said Jeptha Rice, to recover 2060 acres of land, being the amount of Warrant No. 958 issued in the name of his father, the said Jeptha, and which had been located by some person or persons for the University of North Carolina." "The Court decided that they were the heirs of the said Lieutenant Jeptha Rice and adjudged them the title thereto, and a grant No. 25456 was issued for 2560 acres to Baldwin Rice, Levi Smith and Polly, his wife, Henry Rice, William Posea and Elizabeth, his wife, Matthew Rice, Elisha

Gibson and Patsy, his wife, Joseph Rice, Smith and Amy, his wife, and Henry Rice. This land was located in Bardin and McNairy Counties, Tennessee, and a portion of it is now in the possession of some of the children, who reside thereon." "…That he believes an error occurred in the allowance of only sixty dollars per annum to his mother, as that allowance appears to have been made to her as the widow of Jeptha Rice who was a private, and he never understood that his father served as long as one year in that capacity. That his service as a private was performed in the first part of the war, after which as before stated, he was promoted to a lieutenancy and served as such for several years as he always understood from his father, after which and during the latter part of the war, he was appointed quartermaster and in that capacity continued to serve, but for what length of time he is unable to state…"

GENERATION NINE

Hezekiah Benjamin Rice Sr. and Mary Bullock
DOB: 1739 Hanover Co, VA   DOD 1796
Albermarle Co, VA to Caswell Co, NC

Mary Bullock is the daughter of Edward Bullock and Ann Anderson. She was born 1740 in Caswell, North Carolina, USA. Burial 1764 in Mountain View Cemetery, Shrewsbury, MA. She died 1764 in Granville, North Carolina, USA.

Captain Hezekiah Benjamin Rice Sr. and Mary Bullock. They were married 1757 in Virginia, USA. Hezekiah and Mary had 17 children, five died in infancy.

Their children:

Annis Anne (1759-1840) in NC and died in Estill Co, KY

married Capt. John Oldham

Hezekiah Jr. (1764-1860) married Polly Leftwich
  Buried in Rice Family Cemetery in Belton, SC
  1764-1775 lived in Caswell Co, NC. In 1788 he moved to
  Rock Creek, SC and 1805 moved to Hencoop Creek, SC.
  Buried in the Rice Family Cemetery in Belton, SC.

Milly Rice (1757) married John Challes

Othneil Rice (1771-1853) married Sarah (died in Alabama)

Jeptha Rice (1763-1821) married Nancy Joette (lived in Caswell Co, NC and died in Sumner County, TN)

Isban Rice (1763-1847) married Dolly Corless

Edmund Rice (1772) married Henrietta Rice (his 4th cousin)

Nathanial

Elisha 1787

Gideon – he was lame with a swelling in his knee / 2 children:
  Churchwell and Dempsey (Dempsey was lost at sea)

George

John

Hezekiah was born in Virginia (but Welsh in descent) and is listed in the book "Old Families and Churches" by Meade as serving as a vestryman of the Church of England in Fredericksville Parish, Albermarle Co, VA in 1762. He bought land in 1763 and later the same year conveyed the land to John Ritchie. He and Mary were in Orange County, NC before 1771 as he is listed **in Captain Nathaniel Hart's Orange County Militia** (also Caswell Co). He served in the Militia in Virginia in 1775. ,The N. C. House of Delegates appointed Hezekiah Rice of Hillsborough Dist. captain of one of three additional battalions to be raised . References are also made to Hezekiah Rice being a 1st Regt. Lt. and 9th Regt. Capt. He is also mentioned as a captain paid 236 pounds in 1784. Rice's Company organized at Hillsborough, NC under Colonel Ramsey and William Moore.

In 1782 Hezekiah bought land in Caswell County, NC. He entered the Revolutionary War in 1776 and was one of the first Lieutenant's to be appointed for the army and was soon promoted to Captain in the 9t[h] NC Regiment. He died during the Revolutionary War at Santee Hills of small pox. He also fought at Kings Mountain, SC / NC.

It was thought by the War Department that he died without heirs and that he had not served the two year limit of service to receive a land warrant. So in 1821 the land was given to North Carolina University. The children of Jeptha Rice sued in court for the land and established kinship to Hezekiah. It took a few years for Jeptha's family to get the 3840 acres of land due Hezekiah and his heirs. Joseph Rice, son of Jeptha, bought out his siblings claims to the warrant and asked for compensation of money instead of land. About 1852, the government paid Jeptha 12 ½ cents an acre for the 3840 acres. Hezekiah died in 1796 and his son Isban was the executor of the estate. All the sons were named on an 1801 deed when they sold 120 acres of Hezekiah's land in Caswell County, NC on the waters of Hogan Creek.

GENERATION TEN
Benjamin (Benejah) Rice and Mary
DOB; 1710 Hanover Co, VA

Benjamin Rice is the son of William Rice and Elizabeth Lampley. His birth 1710 in Culpepper County, Virginia, Colony (alt. Hanover County, Virginia).

Their Children

Hezekiah Benjamin (1739-1796) married Mary Bullock

Zebulon- Zebulon Rice married Mary (?). Zebulon Rice was
        master to an apprentice named John Carney for the term of
        six years to learn the "art and mystery" of a shoemaker on
        10 August 1754 in Craven County, North Carolina
Benjamin
James d. a 8 Mar 1772 left his land to brother Gideon –
        Craven Co, NC
Evan- d. bt Jun 1806 - Sep 1806 married Jane
Claverly
Ephraim- + d. c 1788 married Rebecca
Gideon - d. c 1803 married sarah and had 12 children

GENERATION ELEVEN

William Rice and Elizabeth Lampley and then Sarah Nelms
DOB: 04-04-1686 (possibly 1720) DOD: 3-1780

Two wives: Elizabeth Lampley married in 1710 and then Sarah Nelms
in 1733
Sarah Nelms was born 1712 in Hampshire, VA. Died 1780
Sarah parents were William Nelms and Elizabeth Bledsoe.

William and Elizabeth's Children:

> **Benjamin 1710-**
> Letticia (1715-
> Hannah Rice (1729) married James Boggs
> David
> William

William and Sarah's Children:

> Ann Rice 1741-1826 (Boone Co, KY) married John Graves
> Richard Rice 1743 Culpepper CO, VA

John 1720-1804 married Mary Finney
Sarah Rice 1747 -1832 married Edward Graves

William Rice was the son of Thomas Rice. Among the early settlers of what is now Culpepper County, was William Rice, who came sometime before the County was organized." Vol. 11, Patent Records, Richmond, VA., p. 120, is a deed from King George II to William Rice for 400 acres in Forks of the Rapid Ann in Orange County. "Beginning at 4 pine on a point on a branch of Dark Run"; deed dated 29 July 1736, signed by William Gooch, Orange County, which at that time included all of Culpepper County, Culpepper County was formed in 1748.

The last will of William Rice was recorded and probated in Culpepper County, 9 February, 1780. Children:

l) Richard 2) Benejah, 3) John, 4) Hannah, 5) Sarah, 6) Ann (wife of John Graves who was to have loan of "1/2 of estate during her natural life); the estate to be equally divided between his children. Executors were: Benejah, John, and Richard Rice, his sons and son-in-law, John Graves

GENERATION TWELVE

Thomas Rice and Ann Marcy Hewes
DOB: 1660 Shirementon, Bristol England DOD: 1711 VA
Bristol, England to Virginia
Ann Marcy Hewes (1664-1722) New Kent, VA

Thomas Rice was our first immigrant to the U.S. His wife was Ann Marcy Hewes. Her father was Robert Marcy and her mother was Jane Plume. She was christened in Leisto, Suffolk, England, 3 November 1632.

Thomas Rice was an apprentice to Capt. John Stevens in 1679. He arrived in Virginia aboard the ship "Bristol Merchant".

He was given a land grant of 1,200 acres by King George II.

He first settled in 1693 in Gloucester County, VA and later bought land in St. Peter's Parish, New Kent County, (later Hanover County). He was a farmer, small plantation owner and some say a medical doctor. He made a trip to England to claim an inheritance and died at sea. Some believe he was assassinated. He was married to Ann Marcy Hewes. When he died at sea, the family did not receive any inheritance and was left destitute. Part of the family moved 30 miles farther up, got a small plantation, raised families and survived. Many were professors of religion.

Thomas's grandson, Rev. David Rice, son of David was known as the Apostle of Kentucky and Father of Presbyterianism. He had moved from Virginia to Kentucky to preach to the new settlers there. David also mentioned his Uncle James, son of Thomas and Marcy walked on crutches for 20 years and was lame. James would ride his horse to visit friends in the country where he found old religious book by Luther and Puritans, which he extracted and read to memory.

Their 15 Children:

Elizabeth Rice married Richard Bennett
Susannah Rice (1699-1785) married Thomas Hart, Jr
> Her son Capt. Nathanial Hart is famous for completing the Watauga land Purchase from the Cherokees. It was the largest Land deal in North America (The Translylvania Purchase

> *Nathaniel Hart was a member of the Transylvania Company and was one of the purchasers of some 20 million acres of land in Kentucky and Tennessee from the Indians in 1775. He was one of the original settlers at Boonesborough in 1775 and helped construct the fort there. Shortly after Thomas Hart's death, his widow Susannah*

Rice and children moved to Orange County and settled on Country Line Creek, where three of her sons--Thomas, Nathaniel, and David--in the late 1750s and early 1760s obtained land grants in the area that was cut off from Orange in 1777 to form Caswell County. Nathaniel Hart's estate, known as Red House, located at Nat's Fork on Country Line Creek, was of considerable proportions.

In 1760 Hart married Sarah Simpson, daughter of Captain Richard Simpson, a large plantation owner who was one of the earliest settlers in what is now Caswell County.

Their daughter, Susanna, in 1783 married General Isaac Shelby, planner of the Battle of Cowpens and hero of the Battle of Kings Mountain, who became the first governor of the state of Kentucky and for whom the towns of Shelby, N.C., Shelbyville, Tenn., and Shelby County, Ky., were named.

Nathaniel and Sarah Hart's grandson, Thomas Hart Shelby of Traveler's Rest, Ky., was said to have been the first importer of thoroughbred livestock, including racehorses, into the state of Kentucky. Hart was appointed a justice of the peace by the royal governor. He served as captain of militia before the outbreak of the Revolution and as captain in the army during the American Revolution. He was killed by Indians near Logan's Station in Lincoln, Ky.

David Rice (1684-1734) married Marcy Searcy -
David and Marcy's son was Rev. David Rice was a famous preacher and known as "The Apostle of Kentucky".
"Pioneer Minister of the Presbyterian Church in KY" and ordained Dec 1763.

Rev David Rice did missionary work in VA, NC, and especially Kentucky. He was known by the title, "The Apostle of Kentucky." He was instrumental in founding Hampton-Sidney College of VA, Transylvania University of KY, and Danville Theological Seminary at Danville, KY. He published several books, including an Essay on Baptism in 1787.

During the Revolutionary War, Rev Rice served as a chaplain and orator to the Hanover militia. In 1792, he was a member of the convention which framed the first constitution of KY. He was the first moderator of the first Presbytery, and the first moderator of the first Synod of KY.

He was a strong supporter of a gradual emancipation of slaves. He and his wife, Mary, were buried in the churchyard of the Danville Theological Seminary where, in 1892, a monument was erected by the Presbyterians of KY to honor his many achievements.

James Rice (1686-1734) married Margaret House
William Rice (1686-1780) married Elizabeth Lampley & Sarah Nelms
Thomas Rice (1688-) married Joyce ? (VA)
Edward Rice (1690-1770) married Ann and is the father of John Rice who married Lettishia (a Cherokee women) and is grandfather of John Rice the indian trader **see story at the end of the book***
Mary Rice (1694) married John Symns
John Rice (1698-1734) married Mary Higgerson
Alice Rice (1700-)
Marcy Rice (1702)
Benjamin (1708) born in VA,
Matthew (1705-1775) married Ann McGeehee. Also Ann Watson.

Prince Edward Co, VA.
Joseph (1711-1765)
Dominick

- **THE INFORMATION BELOW IS WHAT THE MAJORITY OF PEOPLE THINK IS THE CORRECT CONTINUING LINE, BUT THERE ARE DIFFERENT OPINIONS AND RESEARCH.**

GENERATION THIRTEEN
Sir Stephen Rice and Abigail ? or Mary Fitzgerald
DOB: 1637 Dublin, Ireland DOD: 1715
Their Children:

Thomas (1660-1711) rumored to be missing or murdered when returning to England to claim an inheritance
Ibjan (1664-) born Ireland, died Hanover, VA
Hezekiah (1665) Born in Ireland, came to the states with his brothers, rumored to be murdered on his way to Jamestown, VA after selling a tobacco crop.
Dominick
Joseph
David
Edward (1664)

Sir Stephen Rice is Knight of Mount Rice. It is said that Stephen's sons, Thomas and Hezekiah moved to Virginia from England because of the rebellion against King James.

GENERATION FOURTEEN

* Some people think the father of Sir Stephen is Richard Rice, others think it is James Rice and still others are not sure.

Richard Rice and Ann Cooper
(1588-1657) Dingle Ireland and migrated to Virginia

Children: Stephen Rice

GENERATION FIFTEEN

Dominick Rice and Alice Hussey
DOB: 1564 Dingle, Ireland

Alice Hussey was daughter of James Hussey, Baron of Baltrim

Their Children:

> **James (1596) married Elinor White and Phillis Fanning**
> Stephen (1592) Dingle, Ireland
> Andrew (1594-)
> Richard (1588)
> Edward – 1590 Dingle,Ireland
> William married Sarah – had sons Edward and Dominick

GENERATION SIXTEEN

Stephen Rice and Helena Trant
DOB: 1540-1623 Dingle Ireland
Married in 1563 in Ireland.

Helen Trant 1542-1565
Her parents: Thomas Trant

Their Children:

> James – (1564-) was M.P. for Dingle in 1635
> **Dominic – (1564-)also M.P. for Dingle, married Alecia Hussey**
> Dominic had sons William, Stephen and ?

Thomas (1566)

Stephen left all of his holdings to James and Dominick but gave something to the others and recorded all of his children.

Stephen's Rhyming Tombstone:

Stephen Rice Esquire, lies here
A happy life for four score years
Full virtuously he spent
His loyal life, Helena Trant
Who died five years before
Lies here also - Lord Jesus grant
Them life for evermore.

GENERATION SEVENTEEN

Robert Rice and Julianna Whyte
DOB: 1518 Dingle, Ireland DOD: 1569
Married about 1539

Julianna Whyte DOB: 1517 DOD:
    Julianna Whyte's parents were Sir James Whyte, who was the Knight of Cashel County, Tipperary

Their Children:
    Stephen (1540) Dingle, Ireland

GENERATION EIGHTEEN

Edward Rice and Ann Wall
DOB: 1495-1523 Dingle, Ireland
Ann Wall Kerry, Ireland Her parents: John Wall

Their children: Robert,

This is the end of the geneology line.

EXTRA STORIES

Extension story from Edward, son of Thomas Rice and Marcy Hewes
Father: Edward Rice (1690-1752) and mother Ann

Edward and Ann's children : were John (below), Mary and Betty all born in Bertie County, NC

John Rice Sr married Lettishia (cherokee indian)

Children:

Anna – married Daniel Williams – helped brother John with indian trading. Her husbands brother John Williams was the ancestor of famous **playwright Tennessee Williams**

William – also worked for brother John indian trader and William came back to Caswell Co, NC. In 1801 he moved to Franklin Co, IL. Since they were part indian they couldn't own land

Thomas died after 1804 in Caswell Co, NC

Mary married John Rice – one of the County Bucks Ireland line

Nathanial

Elisha – died in 1806 – also helped brother John indian trader

Joel Rice (Caswell Co, NC)

Represented Davidson County in the **NC legislature in 1788** and gain elected to represent the county in the 1789 session held to ratify the U.S. Constitution. A large section of the present TN then belonged to NC. Davidson County is now Nashville, TN. It is believed that Joel's descendants settled in Birmingham, AL and were primarily bankers and lawyers. Joel was the first sheriff of Lauderdale, AL in 1818. He married Mary Pryor Hickman in 1793.

John Rice Jr – 1757-1789 indian trader killed near Clarksville, tn. Scalped and killed by Indians.

Born in Orange Co, NC died 1789 – married Susannah Butler

John moved to Memphis from NC and was known as an old Indian trader. He bought 5,000 acres of land in 1783, which is now Overton Park in Memphis. At one time he had 130,000 acres of land in West Tennessee. Much of this land was unexplored on the Big Hatchie River. The grants were completed after all Indian claims were settled. Judge John Overton and Andrew Jackson (our former President) purchased the Rice lands from their heirs, the Wright family. Later Andrew Jackson sold his shares of the land to General James Winchester and his brother in 1818 for $5,000.

John was centrally headquarted in Nashville and in 1786 was a wealthy man. His two brothers, Elisha and Joel joined him and the three brothers were well known in the Nashville area.
John was friends the famous Valentine Sevier, nephew of General John Sevier. John was killed in January of 1792 going down the Cumberland river with Valentine Sevier and others. It is rumored there was a party of hostile Indians led by the notorious Doublehead. John and his friends were scalped and robbed on the river close to Clarksville, TN. He was buried with Valentine Sevier below the mouth of the Red River.

After Johns' death, brother Elisha was the executor of John's estate, which was heavily and debt and still under Indian claims. Elisha willed large parcels of the land to his siblings and even a parcel for schooling the poor, but the release of the Indian claims took too long. He sold the land against the wishes of his siblings to Attorney John Overton and Overton split the claim with his law partner Andrew

Jackson. They purchased more land from Elisha over the years and John Overton planned and built the city of Memphis.

Litigation among the siblings over the land lasted many years after Elisha's death in 1806. In the end few of the Rice descendants ever received money from the estate.

Elisah also joined John and Joel in Nashville. He married Anne Collier.

SOURCES / REFERENCES

Ancestry.com – census records, death records, land records, military records, marriage records and more.

Rootsweb: Rice-Southern

Photos from Jenny Grissom, part of the Rice family

The Rice-Family News Journal

Find a Grave.com

Tennessee Cousins: A History of Tennessee People by Worth S. Ray, Geneological Publishing Company, Baltimore 1971.

www.ingramcontent.com/pod-product-compliance
Lightning Source LLC
Chambersburg PA
CBHW081417280526
45788CB00009B/3138